in full **Bloom**

Pamela Westland

Photography by David Loftus

SOMA
san francisco

Contents

Many thanks to the following for their help and assistance:
Ocean Home Shopping Ltd, The Pier
Locations: Brett and Elizabeth Gosper, Nicky Hillier

First published in Great Britain in 1998 by Hamlyn, an imprint of Reed Consumer Books Limited. North American edition published 1998 by SOMA Books, by arrangement with Hamlyn.

SOMA / South of Market Books is an imprint of Bay Books & Tapes. For information, address: Bay Books & Tapes / 555 De Haro St., No. 220 / San Francisco, CA 94107.

Library of Congress Cataloging-in-Publication Data:
Westland, Pamela. In Full Bloom: fresh flower arranging in 5 to 30 minutes / Pamela Westland. p. cm. "North American edition"--T.p. verso. ISBN 1-57959-010-1
1. Flower arrangement. 2. Flower arrangement--Pictorial works.
I. Title. SB449.W474 1998 745.92--dc21 97-49014 CIP

Printed and Bound in China
10 9 8 7 6 5 4 3 2 1
Distributed to the trade by Publishers Group West

for Hamlyn:
Publishing Director: Laura Bamford
Creative Director: Keith Martin
Design: Mark Winwood, Ruth Hope
Executive Editor: Simon Tuite
Project Editor: Jane Royston
Production Controller: Peter Thompson
Photography: David Loftus

for SOMA:
Publisher: James Connolly
Art Director: Jeffrey O'Rourke
North American Editor: Melinda Levine
Proofreader: Erika Sloan

Introduction

A vibrant, hand-tied bunch of mixed berries and brilliant blossoms; a trio of spectacular flowers presented in minimalist style; a handful of country-garden flowers clustered together in a teapot – whatever style comes closest to expressing your mood of the moment, you will find creative inspiration for it here.

The concept behind this book is that imagination, flair and even a little courage bring more exciting rewards than time and money; that custom-made containers and specialist floral equipment have their uses, but are not indispensable.

From cover to cover the floral designs show, reassuringly, that the pressure of time is no barrier to creating imaginative displays for a dining or dressing table, windowsill or alcove.

As you become more confident, you could explore the decorations towards the end of the book, the ones that are not stop-watched and second-counted. Spend a little more time emulating the medley of colors, textures and forms that characterize the flower paintings of Old Dutch Masters, or creating a colorful floral wreath that traditionally symbolizes welcome and friendship.

Above all, take time, even if it can only be seconds, to notice each flower. Appreciate beauty through simplicity: the effect of water sprinkled over leaves and petals; the tactile contrasts of spiky seed heads against soft-petaled flowers; and the reflected glory of perfect blooms against harsh, shiny metals. These experiences can be an even greater pleasure than to have time on your hands.

Pamela Westland

In 5 minutes

Crystal clear

What you need...

- Florist's scissors
- Rectangular clear-glass vase

Plant material
- Blue delphiniums
- Pastel pink and white lisianthus blooms

...and some tips!

- Highly polished
Before arranging the flowers, check your vase for marks and,

if necessary, polish it with window-cleaning liquid and a soft cloth.

- Lasting freshness
Flowers positioned underwater will fade more quickly. Lift the stems and pick off these flowers, changing the water at the same time.

- Seasonal variation
Long, straight stems of yellow-flowered forsythia blended with tulips would make an equally attractive grouping in springtime.

Tall stems of ice-blue delphiniums contrast pleasingly here with the supple, gently curving lines of lisianthus in pastel pink and white.

Basic outline

1 Cut the delphinium stems into almost equal lengths. Strip off any leaves that would be below the water-line, but leave on a few of the lowest flowers as these will create an interesting underwater effect. *Arrange the stems in the vase in a crisscross pattern, forming a mesh to hold the lisianthus in place.*

Creating 'movement'

2 Add approximately two-thirds of the lisianthus flowers, positioning them so that they nestle among the framework created by the delphinium flowers and distributing the colors randomly to create a natural appearance. From the remaining lisianthus, select some of the most attractive flowers, cut their stems fairly short and then care-fully arrange them just above the rim of the vase.

The curving lisianthus stems give movement to this design. With its harmonious blend of colors and soft-petaled flowers, the arrange-ment will look best viewed against a cool light – a table in front of a north-facing window would be ideal.

Simply elegant

What you need...

- Plain ginger-jar vase
- Metal pin holder (optional, available from florists)
- Florist's scissors

Plant material
- 3 stems of bird-of-paradise
- 1 or 2 sprays of hypericum (St. John's-wort) berries

...and some tips!

- Balancing act
In a minimalist arrangement, when only a few flowers are used and each one is seen in isolation, an uneven number of stems – three, five or more – generally gives a more pleasing balance to the eye.

- Seasonal variation
A trio of white arums in a rounded, plain vase would make an equally striking composition in spring or summer.

A trio of spectacular bird-of-paradise flowers combined with berries makes for a group that is elegant in its simplicity.

A stem holder

1 Unless the aperture of your chosen container is narrow enough to hold the flower stems firmly, it is advisable to start by placing a metal pin holder in the vase: with its heavy metal base and stout pins, this will steady the top-heavy flowers in the arrangement. *A pin holder like this one can be reused and should last a lifetime.*

Height variation

2 Stand one of the bird-of-paradise flowers against the vase to judge where to cut the first, and longest, stem. Cut at a sharp angle so that it will be able to take up water more readily (this is especially important with thick flower stems such as these – see also pages 132–3). *To achieve a good visual balance and avoid a clash of flowerheads, cut the second stem shorter, and the third stem shorter still. Position the three stems in the vase.*

Front cover

3 With the three principal flowers in place, finish off by adding one or two short sprays of hypericum berries around the rim of the vase. *Keep these stems short – so that the foliage justs rests on the rim – to fill in the aperture without detracting from the simplicity of the group.*

Presented in a cluster of glasses at the table center, or as a single splash of color at each place, roses are ideal for a celebration.

Pink champagne

What you need...

- Florist's scissors
- Wineglasses or glass tumblers (these need not match)
- Craft knife

Plant material
- Roses in a variety of pastel colors (one for each glass)

...and some tips!

- Room for expansion
Check that the glasses or tumblers that you have chosen are wide enough to hold the flowers easily, without squashing them.

- Optical illusion
Hand-blown glass, with its integral pattern of bubbles, is especially effective for this type of presentation – it seems to turn the water into sparkling wine!

- Seasonal variation
Greenhouse carnations are available all year round and, like roses, will take kindly to total immersion. To achieve the best effect, pick off any buds that detract from the simplicity of a single bloom.

Preparation and immersion

1 Cut the rose stems so that the immersed flowerheads will sit just below the rims of the glasses, and strip away all the leaves. Taking each stem in turn – and holding the flower facing away from you – use the craft knife to strip off the thorns, then cut a slit in the end of the stem. Cutting the stem in this way exposes a larger area of plant tissue to water, and so will keep the flowers fresh for longer (see also pages 132–3).

Partly fill each wineglass or tumbler with water and gently press a rose into it. Hold the flowerhead below the water for a few seconds so that the spaces between the petals fill up. *You will be able to create different effects by totally or only partially submerging the flowers – refraction plays pretty visual tricks.*

Just for fun

You don't need a container – just a sense of fun – to create this table decoration that reflects today's trend toward informal entertaining.

What you need...

- Soft, dry cloth
- Florist's scissors
- Skewer (optional)
- Florist's clay (optional)

Plant material
- 3 medium-sized eggplants
- 5 small sunflowers or rudbeckias

...and some tips!

- A firm base
A dab of florist's clay under the eggplants will hold them steady.

- Seasonal variation
In the autumn you could substitute small summer squash, pumpkins or other squashes for the eggplants, decorating them with any large, colorful flowers – dahlias or chrysanthemums would be ideal.

Measuring up and making way

1 Wash the eggplants if necessary, and polish them with the soft cloth until they shine. Decide on the angles that the stems of the sunflowers or rudbeckias will take, and measure each one against the vegetables before cutting. Allow for at least 1½ inches of each stem to be pushed into the eggplant – if you are unsure, err on the long side, as you can trim them later if necessary. Use a skewer (or a stiff, woody plant stem) to pierce holes in the skin of the eggplants.

Piercing the vegetables in this way will avoid putting pressure on the flower stems and the risk of breaking them.

Getting it together

2 Push the sunflower or rudbeckia stems into the ready-made channels in the eggplants. Stand back to assess the effect and, if necessary, recut the stems a little shorter.

If the eggplants appear at all unstable, insert a small strip of florist's clay beneath each one.

1

2

Light fantastic

What you need...

- Long-stemmed wineglass
- Tall, waisted glass vase (or similar)
- Florist's scissors
- Natural-colored raffia
- 2 frosted-glass bottles (optional)

Plant material
- 2 or 3 bunches (depending on vase size) of freesias in mixed colors

...and some tips!

- Special affinity
Frosted-glass and plastic containers of all kinds look very effective with flowers such as freesias, lilies and irises, where petals have a slight sheen.

- Seasonal variation
In spring, you could pair an arrangement of tulips in the larger container (positioning their stems so that they will curve gently outward) with a posy of miniature tulips in the wineglass.

Positioned so that the daylight floods through, glass containers filled with freesias and arranged with frosted bottles make a very pleasing still-life composition.

Using the shape

1 Begin by selecting the straightest freesia stems to make the posy for the wineglass (otherwise it may be difficult to balance), and set these aside. Place the remaining freesias in the vase, creating an airy design so that each one may be viewed separately – this treatment works particularly well with these differently colored flowers.

The outward-curving rim of the blue vase used here dictates a design with freedom of movement, the flower stems curving this way and that to form a circular outline.

An even bunch

2 Gather the reserved freesias loosely into a small bunch and then cut the stem ends level.

When forming the bunch, carefully arrange each of the flowers so that none is crushed or crowded.

A free-standing posy

3 Tie the stems with raffia and then splay out their ends slightly so that the posy stands up securely when you place it in the wineglass.

Position the containers where the daylight will pass through them, adding the frosted-glass bottles to complete the display if you wish.

A group of flowers floating in cool, clear water and left to twist and turn in the breeze makes for very therapeutic viewing on a hot summer's day.

Tranquil pool

What you need...

- Large, shallow stoneware bowl
- Rock chips or small pebbles (or glass nuggets)
- Florist's scissors

Plant material
- Purple-and-white Orchids or white roses

...and some tips!

- Economy wise
Floating Orchid flowers in this way need not be as extravagant as it seems. For example, if you are arranging some long-stemmed

Orchids in a tall container you will probably want to cut off the lowest flowers on the stems, in which case these are the ones to use in your rock pool.

- Single option
An individual flower floating in a shallow bowl beside each place setting makes a lovely decoration for a dinner table.

- Seasonal variation
In the spring months, single, semi-double or double camellias – with their rose like outline and waxy petals – would look extremely effective presented like this.

Natural texture

1 Partially fill the bowl with water and add a handful of the rock chips or pebbles – scattering them randomly – to give the table decoration an added natural dimension.

If the occasion calls for more sparkle, you could use glass nuggets instead, choosing either clear or colored to match the flowers.

Floating flowerheads

2 Cut the flowers from their stems (if using roses, you will also need to carefully pull off any petals that are damaged or discolored). Then simply float the flowers on the water. *There is little point in trying to arrange the flowers in a pattern as the slightest movement or breeze will scatter them in all directions – but that is part of the attraction.*

1

Reflected glory

What you need...

- Florist's scissors
- Tall metal vase
- Protective gloves (optional)
- Small glass vase

Plant material
- 5 red gerbera daisies
- About 8 stems of bear grass

...and some tips!

- **Monochromatic**
The use of a single type of flower, in a single bright color, emphasizes the simplicity of this design and lends oriental overtones.

- **Seasonal variation**
Several white spider or lime-green chrysanthemums, arranged with slender iris leaves, would make a very striking display in the late summer or autumn.

Two contrasting containers, five red gerbera daisies and a handful of bear grasses combine here to create a simple group that has more than usual impact.

Height variation

1 Cut four of the gerbera daisy stems to slightly varying lengths, and place them in the metal vase.

Bear in mind that the composition will have greater sense of movement and visual interest if the flowers face in different directions so that they will be seen from varying aspects.

Gentle curves

2 Always handle the stems of bear grass with great care (or wear a pair of protective gloves to be absolutely safe), as they have painfully sharp edges. Wind the grasses around your hand and hold them there for a few moments; when you release them, they will spring into graceful arcs.

When stored in a shop these grasses tend to flatten out, but winding them around your hand is an easy way to restore their curves and create a natural-looking arrangement.

Double value

3 Add the grasses to the metal vase. Cut short the fifth gerbera daisy stem and place it in the smaller vase, then position the containers so that the single flower is reflected in the metal.

Positioning the two vases in this way will produce two images instead of just one; trailing the strands of bear grass over the smaller vase will serve to unify the composition.

1

Optical illusion

These nosegays of nasturtiums create the illusion that they are growing among the vine tendrils, producing a very natural effect.

What you need...

- Large, shallow stoneware dish
- Florist's scissors

Plant material
- Trails of vine
- Nasturtiums
- Summer squash flowers (if available) or cream-colored monkey-flower *(Mimulus)*

...and some tips!

- Ground level
It should appear as though the flowers are actually growing, not floating in a pond, so be fairly restrained with the amount of water in the dish.

- Well supported
If some of the larger vine leaves submerge into the water and look rather squashed, support them crushed underneath with a few concealed pebbles.

- Seasonal variation
In the early summer, a tangle of clematis stems – complete with some of their flowers and whorls of seed heads – would make another very good subject for this type of treatment.

Gentle ties

1 To make each posy, gather together six or eight nasturtiums and tie the stems loosely with a vine tendril; trim the stem ends if necessary.

Vine tendrils are ideal here, as they will hold the delicate nasturtium stems without cutting into them.

All bunched up

2 Pour a little water into the dish and arrange the trails of vine in the base, letting some leaves overlap the rim. Tuck the completed posies and a few individual nasturtiums and squash flowers (or monkey-flower) among the vine trails, making sure that the stem ends are immersed in the water

For a natural look, arrange the posies and flowers randomly – just as you would find them growing in the wild – rather than in a neat circle or in straight lines.

Celebrate the height of summer with a cluster of gold and lemon sunflowers arranged in a classic vase; this is a design that will look attractive on any surface.

Summer sun

What you need...

- Round, narrow-necked vase
- Florist's scissors

Plant material
- Sunflowers (quantity will depend on vase aperture)
- Trail of hop, vine or ivy

...and some tips!

- Conditioning
If you are able to cut your sunflowers from the garden, you must be sure to condition them as soon as you bring them indoors (see pages 132–3).

- Tying time
If the container that you plan to use has a wide neck, compose the sunflowers into a bunch in your hand, tie the stems with raffia and then lower them into the vase.

- Seasonal variation
To create a similarly bold and beautiful effect in the spring or early summer, you could use orange and yellow lilies or daylilies.

Low level

1 Position the sunflowers that have the shortest stems around the rim of the vase. As you gradually fill in the aperture in this way, the taller stems to be added at the center will be well supported.

When using a single flower like this, placing some of the flowerheads so that they are viewed in profile will give the design a feeling of movement and added interest.

Long trail

2 Add more sunflowers to fill in the center of the group, then add a single trail of foliage to curve across the vase.

If your foliage stem does not have a natural curve, wind it around your hand and leave it there for a minute or so. When you unwind the stem, it should gently curve to complement the roundness of the vase.

Milky-white roses and lisianthus blooms contrast with variegated foliage that spans the color scale from lime-green to a pale lemon, for a look that is sharp and refreshing for summer.

Cool and white

What you need...

- Clear-glass pitcher with straight sides
- Florist's scissors

Plant material
- White roses
- White lisianthus
- Ice plant
- Green (unripe) poppy seed heads
- White phlox
- Variegated pineapple mint
- Feverfew
- Carrot tops or fern fronds
- Small variegated hosta leaves

...and some tips!

- Keeping up appearances
Change the water every day, to ensure that it remains clear. Hold the stems gently in one hand as you pour away the water, let them settle back into place and then pour in fresh water.

- Seasonal variation
In early spring you could create a lovely arrangement using white tulips, cream and pale-green parrot tulips, white narcissus and white bluebells, together with ferns, variegated ivy and a few sage leaves.

Stem support

2 Cut the ice plant stems to varying lengths and arrange them in a cluster in the center, then position more roses around them.

You will find that the network of stems made inititally will hold these later additions firmly in place.

Basic framework

1 Put the choicest two or three roses aside. Make the framework for the design by arranging some of the longest stems – the lisianthus and rose – to crisscross at right angles from opposite sides of the container. *Seen through clear glass, the stems are high profile: let them reach all the way down to the base of the container, as if the finished arrangement could be freestanding.*

(not too many, or their bright yellow centers will be dominant). Finally, add the carrot tops or ferns at the back of the container and the small, solid hosta leaves at the sides.
When using a limited color range of plant materials, it is important to emphasize the contrasting shapes and textures in the arrangement to create visual interest.

Color and texture

3 Position poppy seed heads and phlox flowers among the central cluster, angling some of the stems backward (away from you). Take the roses that you set aside at the start and position them at the center front, where they will act as the focal point of the design. To complete the arrangement, fill in the gaps with pineapple mint and add a few stems of feverfew

Dancing flames

What you need...

- Florist's scissors
- Squat, round cooking pot (or similar)

Plant material
- Pink-orange lilies
- Orange and red gerbera daisies
- Cream roses
- Pampas-grass leaves

...and some tips!

- Handle with care
Pampas-grass leaves have sharp edges, so it is best to wear gloves when handling them, or to do so with

great care. Never run the leaves through your hand in order to bunch them up.

- Lighting up
An arrangement like this, with its blend of pale tints and deep shades, should be seen in a good light to be appreciated.

- Seasonal variation
In the spring, orange-centered daffodils, cream narcissus and orange tulips would make an equally warm composition. In the late summer, you could combine bronze and gold chrysanthemums or dahlias with rowan or hawthorn berries.

Brightly colored lilies and gerbera daisies arranged with cool cream roses in a terra cotta pot create a design that makes just the right accompaniment to a kitchen or barbecue party.

Stem preparation

1 Pull off almost all the leaves from the lily stems, leaving (if you wish) only those that will sit above the water level and be visible.

Removing the leaves from the lower part of the stems will help to keep the water fresh and free from algae.

Good proportions

2 Cut the stems of the lilies so that the lowest flowers rest only just above the rim of the pot as you put them in, then start to intersperse the orange and red gerbera daisies.

Forget anything that you have ever heard about the ideal proportion of plant material to container being in a ratio of two to one – in this case, color and compactness rule!

Good proportions

3 If you would like your roses to be more showy more quickly, gently open out the petals: start at the outside of each flower and work toward the center. Add the roses to the arrangement, recessing some of them close to the pot's rim, then add the pampas-grass leaves in a cluster to one side.

With the roses almost hidden among the lilies, the strong colors of the gerbera daisies will be seen in dramatic silhouette.

A frame of cinnamon sticks resting on the rims of these containers serves to hold the flower stems in place, as well as adding a hint of spice.

Spice is nice

What you need...

- Tumblers and highball glasses
- Cinnamon sticks, each approximately 18 inches long
- Natural-colored raffia
- Florist's scissors

Plant material
- Blue scabious blooms
- Magenta gerbera daisies
- Purple-and-cream Singapore orchids

...and some tips!

- The rustic look
For a more informal display, you could make the triangular frames in the same way but using either straight twigs or lengths of bamboo.

- Seasonal variation
A composition using iris and ranunculus would make an attractive springtime group; later in the year, pale green tobacco plant and pansies would be a pretty alternative.

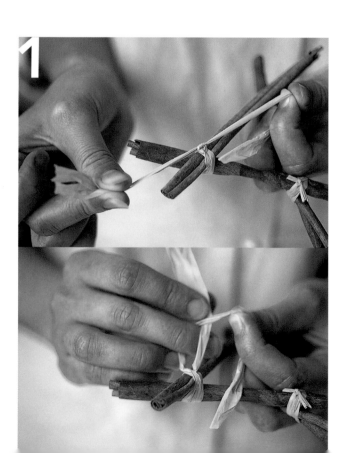

Making the frames

1 To make each frame, break the cinnamon sticks into three equal pieces about 6 inches long. Bind two of the lengths together with raffia, about 1–1/2 inches from the ends. Position the third stick to form a triangle, and bind the sticks at the remaining two crossing points.

You can vary the size of the frames, and of the triangular spaces in the center, according to the size of your containers; the frames are reusable, so you may like to build up a small collection of them in varying sizes.

Bunching up

2 Gather together a small bunch of scabious blooms and gerbera daisies, and cut the stems level. Place one of the frames over a tumbler or high-ball glass and push the stems through the hole.

If you would like the flowers to be more upright – as if the stems had been tied – push the raffia ties inward along the sticks to make the central hole a little smaller.

Dual purpose

3 Long-stemmed flowers such as the orchids used here are especially suited to this type of display. Unless your glasses are colorless, pick off any flowers that would otherwise be submerged in water before you use them, as colored glass may distort rather than enhance their color.

There is no need to waste the low-level flowers – which will be the largest along the orchid stems – that you have removed; you can float them in a stoneware or glass bowl for a beautiful effect (see pages 20–2).

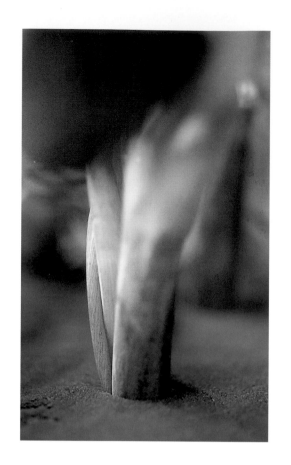

To arrange stems vertically in a wide container, you will need to include florist's foam to hold them securely. Here, the ferns used to line the tank conceal the foam – and they look attractive, too.

Vertical take off

What you need...

- Wide, rectangular glass tank (or similar)
- Block of florist's foam
- Kitchen knife
- Bowl
- Florist's scissors

Plant material
- Shield fern (*Polystichum aculeatum*) or similar
- 2 stems purple gladiolus
- 2 stems blue aga-panthus
- 2 sprays of sea holly (*Eryngium maritimum*) • 1 lime-green chrysanthemum

...and some tips!

- Washing up
If the ferns have gathered any dust in the wild, swish them in warm, soapy water and rinse well before arranging them.

- Moisturizer
To prolong the life of the arrangement, keep the florist's foam permanently moist by filling it up with water each day.

- Seasonal variation
In the springtime, an arrangement of white star-of-Bethlehem (Ornithogalum arabicum), green iris and clusters of yellow-leaved ivy will have great impact.

Preparation

1 Using the kitchen knife, cut the foam block to fit the tank, allowing space all around it to insert the ferns. Soak the foam in a bowl of water for about 20 minutes (or until it sinks to the bottom), then place it in the glass tank. *Slide the ferns between the foam and the glass, and you will see the character of the tank transform into that of a damp forest!*

The principal flowers

2 Cut both the gladiolus stems, one slightly longer than the other, and the agapanthus stems at sharp angles. Arrange the gladiolus stems vertically, with the taller one slightly behind the shorter, and place one agapanthus on either side of the composition. *Used in this way, the round-headed agapanthus will provide a sense of balance and will perfectly complement the spear-shaped gladiolus.*

Diagonal line

3 The sea holly is lighter in color and more wayward than the other flowers: position the two sprays diagonally, so that they trail over the tank rim at the front and back of the design. Finally, place the green chrysanthemum just in view at the back.
Including a surprise element in a flower arrangement is often highly effective; here this is achieved with the sharp lime-green color of the chrysanthemum.

Fruitful idea

What you need...

- Kitchen knife
- Grapefruit knife
- Florist's scissors
- Plate or dish
(for display)

Plant material
- Oranges
- Variegated pineapple mint
- Purple gladiolus
- Orange montbretia
- Purple and cream passion flowers
- Orange marigolds

...and some tips!

- Paintbox colors
Blue and yellow flowers in lemon shells, or red and sharp yellowy green flowers in lime shells would also be good.

- Future use
Once the flowers are over, you can freeze the orange shells for use another time.

- Seasonal variation
Orange miniature tulips arranged in orange shells with grape hyacinths and purple anemones would make a bold and colorful statement in the spring.

Scooped-out orange shells make dramatic containers for a cluster of contrasting flowers. Display them individually or in groups – either way, they are sure to be a focal point.

Container preparation

1 It is not often that foliage and flowers get to drink orange juice, but in this composition they do! Cut a thin slice from the top of one orange (and a sliver from the base if necessary so that the fruit will stand steady), and then use the grapefruit knife to scoop out the flesh from the center. Insert a spray or two of pineapple mint. *Starting with the pineapple mint in this way will help you to define the height of the arrangement.*

Adding color

2 Using a downward movement, carefully pull some of the lower flowers from a stem of gladiolus and arrange it at the front of the orange. Reinforce the line of the pineapple mint with the montbretia stems, add a passion flower, and then fill in the gaps with marigolds and pineapple mint.
Repeat the whole process with the remaining oranges, and arrange them as you wish for display.

Cabbage patch

What you need...

- Kitchen knife
- Florist's scissors
- Decorative plate or dish (for display)

Plant material
- Savoy cabbage
- 2 Star lilies

...and some tips!

- **Conditioning**
The cabbage will not provide the lilies with a moisture source, so leave them in water for as long as you can before arranging them. After the event, put them in water again – it will take only moments to re-create the decoration another time.

- **Show time**
If you wish to use flowers other than the Star lilies, choose large, showy blooms – clusters of small flowers would look insignificant against the heavily textured cabbage.

- **Seasonal variation**
In the late summer or autumn, a red cabbage (having been stripped of any discolored outer leaves) would make a dramatic and unusual container for pink and green hellebores, or for pink bearded iris.

Whatever your choice of dishes for an informal gathering, put cabbage on the menu in this highly unusual way.

Initial preparation

1 Cut a sliver from the base of the cabbage so that it will stand steady on the plate or dish. Cut one lily stem a short distance below the lowest flower, and strip off the lower leaves (if kept in the arrangement, these would wilt more quickly than the flowers).

This is more than ever a design that encourages freedom of expression, so there is no ideal length for the displayed stems; however, remember that they will make the decoration top-heavy if left extra long.

Flower decoration

2 Cut the discarded piece of stem to a sharp angle at one end, and use it to pierce holes in the cabbage. *Carefully push the cut lily stem into a ready-made hole – you will find that the cabbage is more receptive to the stem than you might imagine.*

Extra texture

3 Cut the lowest flowers from the second lily stem and insert these short stems around and below the central stem. You can insert them at any angle – even sloping downward. *If you wish, cluster together a trio of leaves and insert them behind the main stem to add textural variety.*

Checking out

What you need...

- Florist's scissors
- Round, bulbous checked pitcher

Plant material
- 5 or 6 cream Brompton stocks
- Cream, pale pink, mauve and purple lisianthus (quantity required will depend on size of pitcher)
- 3 bright pink roses

...and some tips!

- Color balance
Blending flowers as contrasting in color as the cream and purple of this pitcher can be very difficult, but halfway tones and tints such as the pinks and mauves used here will help to bridge that gap.

- Seasonal variation
In the spring you could substitute blue or white bluebells for the long-stemmed Brompton stocks, and place pale and vibrant ranunculus blooms around them.

The blue and white design of a boldly checked pitcher is echoed – and then diluted – by a selection of flowers that includes lisianthus in a range of four coordinating shades.

Handheld

1 Cluster the stocks in one hand. Arrange the various colors of the lisianthus around the stocks, keeping these flowerheads slightly lower than the tips of the central flowers; then add the three pink roses in a cluster, with their stems shortest of all.

Composing an arrangement in the hand like this is a quick and easy way to achieve a free, natural look in a wide-necked container.

More of the same

2 Continue adding lisianthus around the posy in your hand. Hold the posy against the pitcher to check it for height, then cut the stems level.

Hold the stems gently but firmly, being careful not to crush any of the flowers as you trim the ends.

Letting go

3 Place the posy in the pitcher, with the roses at the front. Release the stems from your hand and allow them to settle into place.

Stand back to assess the arrangement and, if necessary, use both hands to ease the flowers very gently so that none of them are crushed or at an awkward angle.

Daisy shapes

What you need...

- Florist's scissors
- Goldfish bowl (or similar)

Plant material
- Trails of hop, vine or ivy
- Approximately 12 yellow gerbera daisies
- 1 red gerbera daisy

...and some tips!

- All change
Change the water in the bowl if it becomes cloudy. Recutting the stem ends of the flowers at the same time will considerably prolong their life.

- Seasonal variation
In winter, try making an arrangement of yellow, silver and deep green foliage – including glossy evergreens such as laurel, bay and Elaeagnus – with some lavender and cotton lavender for contrast. One or two waxy-textured flowers – such as hellebores or camellias – tucked in among the stem-holding foliage would make a very pretty finishing touch.

Long trails of hop wound inside this bowl act as natural stem-holders for the gerbera daisies; vine or ivy leaves can be used just as easily.

Making a base

1 If necessary, wash the foliage in warm, soapy water and then rinse it thoroughly. Cut off any thick or woolly stems that would cloud the water. Wind the hop, vine or ivy stems around the inside of the bowl.

As you wind the foliage, ease out some of the largest leaves so that they are clearly visible against the glass — any crushed leaves will look ugly.

Building in height

2 Arrange short stems of the yellow gerbera daisies around the edge of the bowl, allowing some of them to droop over its rim for a natural effect.

Build up the height of the arrangement with longer stems in the center, to create a domed shape.

Helping hands

3 Tuck in the red gerbera daisy among the yellow flowers. Continue building up the arrangement with yellow gerbera daisies, placing longer stems at the center to create the attractive domed effect.

Once you have added all the flowers, ease them gently into place and reposition any stems that have not stood firm among the foliage trails.

In 10 minutes

1

Greenish pink hydrangea heads need little in the way of embellishment here, with the exception of a few greenish yellow fennel seed heads.

All the greens

What you need...

- Florist's scissors
- Craft knife
- Round basket with water-holding inner container

Plant material
- Green and pink hydrangea
- Fennel seed heads

...and some tips!

- Aromatherapy
The fragrance of the fennel seed heads will enhance this composition; dill and caraway are other options. Just to touch these seed heads is to enjoy them!

- Everlasting
After use, dry the hydrangeas for long-lasting decorations: stand them in a dry container in a warm place, or stand in 2 inches of water at room temperature and let dry.

- Seasonal variation
In late summer or autumn, you could achieve a similar domed effect using either mop-headed chrysanthemums or dahlias, arranged with yarrow.

2

Measuring and cutting

1 Strip away the lower leaves from the hydrangea stems (you could use these separately in another arrangement). Measure the height of the stems against the basket, and cut them at an angle. Using the craft knife, slit the ends and scrape off the woody bark.
When measuring the stems against the basket, remember that you want the flowers to form a rounded dome shape – not a flat surface.

In-filling

2 Position the hydrangea stems in the basket so that they overlap its rim in places, and then arrange the fennel seed heads to fill in any gaps.
Check to make sure that the inner container is not visible from any viewpoint – even through the basket handles – and, if necessary, add more seed heads to conceal it.

1

Token of love

What you need...

- Craft knife
- Florist's scissors
- Natural-colored raffia, or ribbon

Plant material
- Asters in mixed colors
- White roses
- Pink thistle flowers
- Purple lisianthus

...and some tips!

- Water shortage
Give all the flowers a long drink of cool water and keep them in a cool place before you arrange them.

- Flower meanings
To make your posy more meaningful, you could use flowers that in Victorian times carried a particular message, as found in flower-language dictionaries. Asters, for instance, meant "a variety of emotions"; white roses said "I am worthy of you."

- Seasonal variation
Flowers available all year round – such as greenhouse-grown carnations and spray carnations – mixed with ferns and ivy leaves would make a very pretty posy. Deep-red carnations signify true love; ferns mean sincerity; and ivy, fidelity.

A small posy of delicate pastel flowers tied to a bedpost, placed on a pillow or hung in a doorway will evoke more than a hint of Victorian romance and welcome.

Preparation

1 Strip the lower leaves from the asters and all the leaves from the rose stems, using the craft knife to remove any thorns.

Removing the leaves will give the finished posy a neat appearance.

Head height

2 Gather in one hand a cluster of pink thistle flowers (these will be the longest in the posy), and begin to add the asters. Add more and more rings of asters, the heads of each new layer slightly below those in the previous one. Make sure that the flowers are not too crowded, or crushed. You could compose the bunch in color order – forming a ring of pink flowers, then a ring of blue, and so on – but a random approach will have greater spontaneity. It will help to fluff out the flowers with your hand as you compose the bunch, and to loosen the stems slightly if your grip seems too tight. Add the purple lisianthus

stems at the sides of the posy, where they will define its shape, and position the white roses in a cluster at the center front. Cut the stems of all the flowers level, then tie them neatly with a length of raffia or ribbon.

Hang the posy wherever you like: above a door, it would signify a welcome to party guests; tied to a bedpost, it will perhaps have a more personal significance.

Floral fruit bowl

What you need...

- Wide, deep pottery dish
- 4 or 5 water-holding flower vials (available from florists)
- Florist's scissors
- Craft knife

Plant materials
- Yellow and white roses (quantity will depend on size of dish)
- Greenplums
- Lady's-mantle

...and some tips!

- Improvisation
Instead of flower vials, you could use small plastic pillboxes or tiny bottles with holes pierced in the lids to insert the rose stems. Alternatively, simply give the flowers a good drink of cool water and then wrap their stems in damp paper towels.

- Seasonal variation
Small green apples – arranged with orange zinnias, and clusters of rowan berries and rosehips – would make a striking winter table decoration.

Fruit and flowers are made for one another in this simple partnership of greenplums and roses; they are also given a soft trim of lady's-mantle.

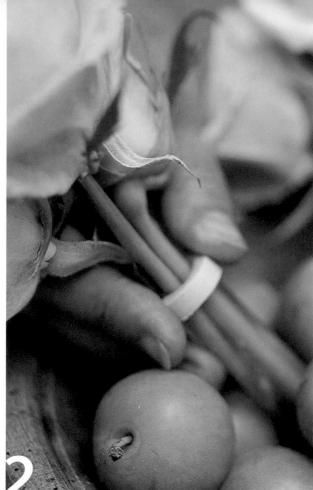

Hidden assets

1 Partially fill the flower vials with water. Cut short the rose stems, use the craft knife to strip off any thorns and push two or three stems into the hole in each vial cover.

Carefully adjust the roses, using your fingers, so that the flower heads are at varying levels and do not crush one another.

Adding color

2 Partially fill the dish with greenplums and then press the flower vials down among the fruit, angling them this way and that.

Arrange at least one of the flower clusters so that it overlaps the rim of the dish and visually breaks up its hard outer edge.

Adding substance

3 Fill up the dish with the remaining greenplums so that the flower vials are completely hidden; finish off by tucking a few stems of lady's-mantle in a cluster around one flower group.

The soft, blurred outline of this mass of tiny flowers will make a pleasing shape and texture contrast to the roundness of the plums and the smooth rose petals.

Moody blues

A hand-tied bunch of flowers in a mix of complementary colors is blended here with rich blue hydrangea heads to flatter a wide-necked vase.

What you need...

- Natural-colored raffia
- Florist's scissors
- Round, wide-necked vase

Plant material
- Orange and pink snapdragon
- Dark blue larkspur
- Purple lisianthus
- Peach and orange roses
- Blue hydrangeas

...and some tips!

- Revivalist tactics
Hydrangea flowers will benefit from the hot-water treatment. Immediately after cutting the stems, immerse the ends in boiling water for a few seconds (be sure to protect the flower-heads from steam with a cloth), and then stand them in cold water to revive.

- Seasonal variation
In the summer, you could fill the front of a design similar to this one with clematis flowers, using lupins and knotweed in mixed colors to provide height, and perennial cornflowers and pyrethrum chrysanthemums for the round shapes.

Handmade

1 Cut a piece of raffia long enough to fit around all the flower stems in a loop, and put it aside. Arrange the snapdragons and larkspur stems in a group in one hand, interspersing the lisianthus blooms (with their heads positioned a little lower), and adding the roses in a ring around the bunch. *Your aim is to compose a bunch with the flower heads becoming gradually lower toward the front – just as they might grow in a flower border.*

Height check

2 When you have formed the bunch to your satisfaction – turning it around in your hand to check that the finished design will look equally good from whatever angle it is seen – take up the precut length of raffia in your free hand, then loop and tie it around the flower stems. Hold the bunch up against the vase and check it for height before cutting the stems. *You will want the lowest flowers to be only slightly higher than the hydrangeas, so think about this before you cut the stems.*

Final composition

3 Place the tied bunch in the vase, carefully easing out the stems with your fingers so that the flowers are freestanding. Add the hydrangeas to fill the front of the vase. *Stand back to assess the completed arrangement, making any minor positioning adjustments as necessary.*

Lime-green chrysanthemums are wonderfully showy flowers, and are "planted" here in a pot with small, contrasting blooms to create a faux topiary.

Flower tree

What you need...

- Flowerpot and water-holding container to fit inside
- Florist's clay (available from florists), or modeling clay
- Small metal pin holder (optional)
- Florist's scissors
- Craft knife

Plant material
- 1 lime-green chrysanthemum
- 2 or 3 stems of lime-green miniature spray chrysanthemums
- Purple lisianthus

...and some tips!

- Suitable material *When selecting flowers to display in this way, choose those with straight, sturdy stems that will best represent the tree-trunk effect.*

- Container wise *Experiment with containers made of various materials to create widely different results. Aluminium flower pots, frosted-glass pots, and others that have been painted and/or stenciled will all alter the character of the presentation.*

- Seasonal variation *In the early summer, a large, ball-shaped geranium flower in red, pink, peach or white would make a delightful centerpiece surrounded by pink and white daisies or cornflowers.*

A secure base

1 To secure the principal flower –
the green chrysanthemum – so that
it has a moisture source, press a strip
of florist's clay (a material that stays
in position, even in water) to the
underside of the pin holder and then
press this into the inner container.
*Alternatively, as the chrysanthemum
will last reasonably well out of water,
you can simply secure the stem in a
ball of modeling clay pressed into the
container before filling it with water.
The main stem will then not be able
to take up water, but the other flowers will do so.*

Blossoming out

2 If the chrysanthemum is not fully
open, ease it to a fuller shape by
gently pressing the petals outward
with thumb and forefinger. Measure
the flower against the pot for height,
cut the stem and "plant" it in the pot.
*Once you have cut the stem to
length, use the craft knife to split
it if you are going to put it in water.*

Mix and match

3 With the chrysanthemum firmly
in place, surround it with short stems
of spray chrysanthemums.
*These lime-green sprays match the
color of the chrysanthemum perfectly, forming a visual link.*

Color contrast

4 One by one, carefully add the purple
lisianthus flowers around and between
the spray chrysanthemums.
*The finished decoration resembles
a neatly clipped evergreen tree rising
from a colorful bed of flowers.*

Salad days

What you need...

- Knife
- Citrus-fruit zester
- Glass plate (or similar moisture-proof holder)

Plant material
- 1 cucumber
- Sprays of rowan berries
- Red geraniums
- Trails of Russian vine
- Maidenhair fern

...and some tips!

- Vegetable craft
Experiment with cutting away the cucumber skin to make other patterns, such as hearts, diamonds, daisies or any other simple shapes. A craft knife will be best suited to this task.

- Seasonal variation
Bright red poppies and sweet peas – with golden leaves such as oregano or thyme – would make a stunning presentation in the height of summer.

Chunks of cucumber have all it takes to display flowers and foliage: an interesting texture, plenty of moisture and the all-important element of surprise.

Container preparation

1 Cut off the ends of the cucumber. Cut the remainder into three unequal lengths, and then scrape the zester firmly down the length of each section to make ridges all around it.

There is no need to keep the ridges even: in fact, you may find irregular light and dark stripes on these cucumber vases more attractive.

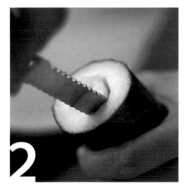

Voilà!

2 Use the knife to scoop a hole in the top of each cucumber section. Check, too, that the bottoms are flat and that the sections will stand straight. Fill each of the "vases" in turn with a mix-and-match selection of bright scarlet rowan berries and geranium flowers, contrasted with dainty Russian vine trails and maidenhair fern fronds. Allow some of these materials to trail over the sides of the containers, as this will make the decorations look more natural and, therefore, more visually appealing.

You can arrange the filled cucumber sections either in a cluster as a centerpiece, or individually – perhaps using one at each place setting around the table.

1

Country casual

What you need...

- Florist's scissors
- Ceramic pitcher in a bold color

Plant material
- Lady's-mantle
- Peach, pale pink and dark pink roses
- Blue delphiniums
- Mauve lisianthus blooms
- Lime-green spray chrysanthemums
- Light and variegated pineapple mint

...and some tips!

- Extending vase life
When blending a mix of flowers that have different lasting properties – here, for instance, the roses are likely to go over most quickly – you should discard any that fade and replace them with fresh ones.

- Seasonal variation
As a springtime alternative, bring together pale pink and white daffodils, apricot tulips, blue and white lilac, grape hyacinth and variegated ivy to make a beautiful arrangement with quite a different feeling.

At the height of summer, this colorful collection of country-garden flowers will bring a hint of nostalgia to any setting.

Trimming down

1 Begin by preparing all the materials, trimming the stem ends and removing any leaves low on the stems.

Trimming will only be approximate at this stage, but be careful not to cut stems too short – measure them first against the height of the pitcher.

Networking

2 Arrange the lady's-mantle stems from either side of the pitcher so that they crisscross just below the rim and form a mesh to hold other materials in place. Start to add the other flowers, beginning with the roses and spacing them evenly within the mesh.

The misty effect of the tiny lady's-mantle flowers will soften the outline of the finished design, and appear to tone down the stronger colors.

Color build-up

3 Add the remaining roses, and the delphinium and lisianthus blooms, distributing the stronger colors evenly. Arrange stems of light-colored and variegated pineapple mint to trail down over the pitcher's rim.

The arrangement should look random and natural, as if you had gathered the flowers one by one from a garden. Trailing the pineapple mint will separate the stronger tones and break up the solid color of the pitcher, unifying the flowers and their container.

Beads of color

What you need...

- Glass container for mixing
- Bowl
- Blue food coloring
- Old spoon
- Water-retaining crystals (available from garden centers and specialty stores)
- Glass vase
- Florist's scissors

Plant material
- Bird-of-paradise flowers

...and some tips!

- Storage and reuse
Store any unused colored water in a closed container. As the plant stems draw water from the crystal, you can then refill it with additional colored water in order to keep them moist and to prolong the life of the flowers.

- Seasonal variation
In winter, one or two bright red poinsettias would make a striking presentation, perhaps supported by crystals tinted with green food coloring.

Water-holding crystals are normally used in planted tubs and hanging baskets. In a glass pitcher, they can be colored blue – or any other shade – to create the brightest stem-holding material you are likely to see.

Coloring crystals

1 Fill the glass container with cold water, and stir in a few drops of food coloring. Spoon some of the crystals into the bowl and then pour in some colored water. The crystals can absorb several hundred times their own weight in water and, as they do so, will swell into soft, round beads.

Gradually stir more water into the container until the crystals are thick enough to support the flower stems. Then, transfer to the vase.

Flower arranging

2 Cut the bird-of-paradise stems at a sharp angle and to slightly different lengths, and then arrange them in the holding material.

Cutting the stems at an angle will enable them to take up more water; arranging them at different heights will give the design a greater feeling of movement and variety. Also the beaks of the birdlike flowers will be less likely to touch.

Victorian style

What you need...

- Plain china pitcher
- Florist's scissors

Plant material
- Blue delphiniums
- Mauve, red and pink asters
- Pink Peruvian lilies
- Peach and red geraniums
- Orange and bronze zinnias
- Scented geranium leaves
- Sprays of viburnum foliage

...and some tips!

- Color choices
An arrangement in an all-white or cream jug will look best if at least one flower group is pale to medium in tone; an all-dark composition in a container of this color would look top-heavy and unbalanced.

- Seasonal variation
Gather together a medley of forsythia, ranunculus, tulip and lilac to make a scented springtime arrangement.

Blue and mauve, red and pink, peach, orange and bronze: this composition presents a medley of bright, vibrant colors in the true Victorian tradition.

Color concentration

1 Arrange the delphinium stems in a ring around the back of the jug, where they will define the height of the arrangement. Gather a handful of mauve asters, followed by some of the pink Peruvian lilies, and add these in bunches. Continue in this way with the red and pink asters and with more lilies.

Adding the flowers in this way, color by color, emphasizes the gradual progression through the arrangement from the blue and purple shades on to the pinks and reds. This helps to create a natural yet ordered effect, characteristic of the Victorian approach.

Color buildup

2 Position the geranium flowers close to the front rim of the pitcher, and then arrange the zinnias individually among the vibrant colors of the asters. Lastly, tuck in individual geranium leaves and sprays of viburnum.

Arranging the darker zinnias separately among clustered groups works well here (using pastel flowers in this way could have produced a spotted look).

Natural beauty

What you need...

- Kitchen knife
- Florist's scissors

Plant materials
- 1 watermelon
- Magenta dahlias
- Freesias in purple and mixed colors

...and some tips!

- **Toning up**
However casual a decoration, it will be more effective if the color of one of the flowers coordinates with the color of the holder – in this case, with the pinky flesh of the fruit.

- **Keeping fresh**
Although the flowers will have a moisture source, the watermelon will not keep fresh for many days at room temperature. Remove the flowers at night and put them in water, cover the melon with plastic wrap and put it in the refrigerator – and then rearrange the flowers in the morning.

- **Seasonal variation**
A pumpkin burgeoning with bronze chrysanthemums or dahlias, cream roses and orange rowan berries could take center stage at any autumn-harvest celebration or Thanksgiving dinner.

Watermelon is not only visually attractive and highly refreshing to eat – it can also make one of the prettiest flower containers you are ever likely to use.

Standing securely

1 Using the knife, cut a thin slice
from the top of the watermelon and,
if necessary to make it sit securely,
cut a thin piece from the base as well.
*If you cut from the bottom of the
melon, you will obviously need
to stand it on a waterproof base in
order to protect your furniture.*

Changes of direction

2 Cut the dahlia stems to varying
lengths and press them into the top
of the melon, with the flowers facing
in different directions.
*As the sliced top of the watermelon
is so pretty, make sure that you don't
hide it beneath a mass of flowers.*

Working in clusters

3 With the dahlias in position, arrange
a cluster of purple freesias on one side
of the melon, then add another group
of freesias in mixed colors opposite
and toward the back.
*Concentrating the color in one
of the flower groups in this way will
give even more impact to your light-
hearted and informal decoration.*

Kumquats floating in a decorative glass vase act as unofficial stem holders, and make an interesting study of color and texture beneath the flowers.

Floating fruit

What you need...

- Florist's scissors
- Tall glass vase

Plant material
- Orange Peruvian lilies
- Sprays of hypericum berries
- Orange and bronze zinnias
- 1 yellow lily
- Kumquats

...and some tips!

- Keeping fresh
Change the vase water frequently (as soon as it starts to look cloudy): it must be kept sparkling for an arrangement like this to look effective.

- Seasonal variation
Pale green gooseberries floating in a clear glass vase, arranged with long spires of bells-of-Ireland, yellow snapdragons and yellow marigolds, would make a very attractive design to celebrate the arrival of spring.

1

2

Preparation

1 Partially fill the vase with kumquats, then pour in some water. Prepare all the plant materials: strip the lower leaves from the Peruvian lilies, cut the hypericum and zinnia stems to varying lengths, and cut the yellow lily stem fairly short (this will be at the front). *Measure the stems against the vase height before cutting; if necessary, you can then make additional adjustments as you arrange them.*

Stem formation

2 Arrange some of the Peruvian lilies from either side so that their stems cross below the level of the fruit. Arrange hypericum stems at different heights among the lilies, angling some of the stems forward to give the arrangement depth, and add more lilies as required. Arrange the zinnia stems in twos and threes throughout the group. Lastly, position the yellow lily close to the vase rim, where it will become the focal point. *Although the lily is a key feature of the composition, when you place the arrangement on a table or on a windowsill, do not feel that this flower must face directly forward – it can be better to avoid the obvious.*

Tea blending

What you need...

- Natural-colored raffia
- Florist's scissors
- Plain teapot

Plant material
- Purple and mauve verbena
- Scented geranium leaves
- Peony foliage
- Pink Peruvian lilies
- 1 yellow lily
- Pink-flowering ice plant

...and some tips!

- Color opposites
In order to create the strongest color contrasts, you can combine any two colors that sit opposite each other on the color wheel. Mauve – a blend of primary red and blue – is opposite primary yellow, which is why the verbena posy looks so striking in this yellow teapot.

- Seasonal variation
In spring, the yellow teapot could blossom with yellow ranunculus and mauve and purple lilac; an orange teapot would look at its most vibrant filled with orange-centered daffodils and narcissus, bluebells and grape hyacinths.

A posy of purple and mauve verbena is blended with pastel-colored lilies in an arrangement that contains elements of both the traditional and the modern; a sunny yellow teapot makes the perfect container.

Exploiting color

1 Gather the purple and mauve verbena into a posy, and back it with scented geranium leaves. Tie the stems with raffia and cut them level. Position a peony leaf at the back of the teapot – where it will frame the flower group – and add some of the (less open) Peruvian lilies, followed by the yellow lily, placing this at the front of the teapot and just above its rim. *Keeping the small verbena flowers in a cluster will concentrate the strong, vibrant color in one area. In contrast, the sharp color of the lemon-yellow lily almost merges with the container, and in turn gives greater prominence to the more delicately colored lilies.*

Textural contrast

2 Arrange a cluster of fully opened Peruvian lilies at the center of the teapot, with the ice plant flowers around them. Insert the verbena posy at the front of the design. *The almost beadlike texture of the ice plant heads will complement the soft outlines of the Peruvian lilies in their similar colors.*

This combination of soft fruit and summer flowers in strawberries-and-cream colors makes for a table centerpiece that is quite irresistible.

Strawberry fair

What you need...

- Glass tumbler
- Footed glass bowl
- Florist's scissors

Plant material
- Strawberries
- Cream Brompton stocks
- Cream, peach, pale pink and deep pink roses
- Cream and pink lisianthus
- Cream scabious
- Pink godetia
- Bear grasses

...and some tips!

- **Perfect balance**
Aim to keep the overall impression of the flower group light and airy, or the completed arrangement may look out of balance.

- **Seasonal variation**
*When soft fruit is out of season, consider other materials: mixed nuts polished until they shine; small duck or quail eggs combined with sea holly (*Eryngium maritimum*) and globe thistles; colored pebbles or shells with a group of statice, sea lavender and strawflower blooms.*

Setting up

1 Carefully place the tumbler in the center of the glass bowl, and then fill the tumbler with water.

Make sure that the tumbler is firmly balanced, and not likely to wobble.

A firm base

2 Partially fill the space between the two containers with whole strawberries.

The fruit will not only give interest and color to the arrangement, but also helps to keep the glass tumbler steady and secure.

Clusters of color

3 Establish the height of the flower group with three stems of cream stocks. Keeping the deep pink roses to one side, arrange groups of the remaining roses and the lisianthus blooms color by color, keeping the flowerheads well below the height of the stocks. Cut the scabious stems so that you can arrange the flowers in a ribbon through the design.

Selecting the pale-colored stocks to be the tallest in the group will prevent the design from looking top-heavy, while the neutral tone of the scabious will separate the other pale tints and highlight each one.

Side interest

4 Carefully insert a cluster of the deep pink roses on one side of the arrangement.

These roses – which provide the strongest color of all – will have a much greater impact when grouped together in this way.

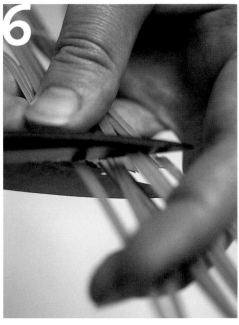

Balancing act

5 Arrange the pink godetia – again, in a cluster – on the opposite side of the arrangement to the roses.

This second flower group – which is also strong in color – balances the effect of the roses, with the combination providing visual weight at the base of the arrangement.

Gentle curves

6 Gather together several stems of bear grasses, measure them against the decoration and then cut them to length. Insert the stems at one side of the tumbler, adjusting their position so that they fan out beautifully.

To enhance the natural shape of the bear grasses, wrap them around your hand and hold them there for a few moments to restore their curves.

1

A silver-colored wire basket arranged with creamy white flowers is worthy of a special family celebration such as a wedding or a baptism.

Precious metal

What you need...

- Oval wire basket with handle
- Water-holding container to fit inside basket
- Florist's scissors

Plant material
- Long ivy trails
- Variegated sage
- White scabious
- White roses
- White lisianthus
- Lady's-mantle

...and some tips!

- A new look
For a completely different appearance, fill the space between the basket and the water-holding container with crumpled tissue paper in white or another soft shade.

- Seasonal variation
For a celebration in the spring months, you could create a similar arrangement using pale green hellebores, white tulips, daffodils and bluebells, with a base of variegated ivy.

Filling the basket

1 Wind ivy trails to fill the gap between basket and inner container, then wind more trails to fill the container and form a natural stem holder.

Survey the basket from all angles to make sure that the container is completely hidden.

Gradual buildup

2 Tuck in short sprays of the lime-green sage among the ivy to make a lighter base, and then add short stems of scabious to form a ring that defines the outer rim of the basket. Cut the rose stems short, and add these and then the lisianthus within the existing oval outline.

Your aim here is to achieve a gradual buildup of height towards the center of the arrangement, thus creating a shallow dome shape.

Sharp contrast

3 Fill in the design with short sprays of lady's-mantle, allowing some of this to spill over the basket rim.

The misty sprays of tiny lime-green flowers will separate the white blooms, emphasizing the contrasting textures of each one.

20 minutes

1

Flower rings

What you need...

- Round bowl or dish
- Transparent tape
- Florist's scissors
- Florist's watering can, or funnel

Plant material
- Yellow gerbera daisies
- Blue scabious blooms
- 1 lime-green chrysanthemum

...and some tips!

- Old-fashioned style
You could compose an arrangement to resemble a Victorian posy, by making a larger number of concentric rings of small flowers in contrasting colors.

- Seasonal variation
An arrangement on a smaller scale – consisting of pansies, buttercups and daisies in a shallow glass dish – would make a charming composition in the early spring.

For this bright concoction, the container is arranged with rings of contrasting flower heads, which are cleverly supported using a well-hidden framework of transparent tape.

The framework

1 Working from one side to the opposite side of the bowl or dish, place strips of tape parallel to one another and approximately 1¼ inches apart.

Complete the crisscross framework by placing strips of tape from side to side, at right-angles to the first set of strips.

Watering holes

2 Using a watering can with a long, narrow spout (or a funnel), partially fill the bowl or dish with water.

Pour the water carefully: if you keep the structure dry, you will be able to reuse it indefinitely.

Outer ring

3 Cut the gerbera daisy stems so that the ends will come below the water level when you arrange the flowers. The stems shown are about 3 inches long, but the appropriate length will depend on the depth of your bowl or dish. Arrange the daisies in a ring around the bowl, pushing the stems through the holes in the framework.

The flowers should overlap the container rim and just touch one another, edge to edge – any gaps would give away the secret of their clever support system!

Color contrast

4 Cut the scabious stems to a uniform length and arrange these flowers edge to edge in a ring inside the circle of gerbera daisies. *Once again, make sure that there are no gaps between the flower heads as this will spoil the effect.*

Flower center

5 For the finishing touch, position the green chrysanthemum at the center of the arrangement. *If the flower is not yet fully open, gently ease out the petals with your fingers and thumbs to make it into a more rounded shape.*

Hand-tied bunch

What you need...

- Craft knife
- Green twine
- Florist's scissors
- Purple or mauve tissue paper
- Clear cellophane
- Wide purple ribbon
- Narrow mauve ribbon
- Bucket or other dry container

Plant material
- Ruby and pink roses
- Purple freesias
- Sea holly (*Eryngium maritimum*)
- Sprays of viburnum
- Hypericum (St. John's-wort) berries
- Whitebeam (*Sorbus aria*) berries

...and some tips!

- Practice run
Composing a hand-tied bunch is easy when you know how, but you may like to practice initially with some inexpensive flowers and foliage before embarking on a special gift posy.

- Seasonal variation
A hand-tied bunch composed of a single flower type – even in a single color – can be as good as any medley of form and texture. In the spring, tulips and parrot tulips arranged with a few of their leaves and slender bear grasses look especially pretty presented in this way.

Say it with flowers in perhaps the prettiest way of all, with a hand-tied posy that anyone would be thrilled to receive. After a little practice, you will find this very easy to make.

Conditioning

1 Prepare all the plant materials with special care (see pages 132–3), as they may be out of water for several hours. Using the craft knife, strip off all the rose thorns and pull away the lower leaves; scrape the bark from the ends of woody stems and slit them. *If any of the flowers (or foliage) start to wilt, revive them by immersing the ends in boiling water for a few seconds, then give all the materials a good long drink in cold water, in a cool place, away from strong light. Care taken at this stage will really pay dividends later.*

Starting point

2 Arrange the flower and foliage stems in groups so that you can easily pick up each one without getting them into a tangle. Have the twine ready for tying. Take two roses in one hand so that their stems cross. Give them a quarter-turn in your hand, then add two more roses, one facing to the left and the other to the right. Add more stems, beginning with the freesias. *This is the method to follow all the way through: a quarter-turn, two more stems crossing in opposite directions and another quarter-turn, followed by more stems, and so on.*

Color variation

3 Add more stems in the same way, contrasting colors and textures all the time. Purple freesias and sea holly will, in their different ways, contrast strikingly with the velvety roses, and whitebeam and hypericum berries introduce yet more textural interest. *Arrange the flower heads or foliage tips of each layer only slightly lower than the previous layer: the finished bunch should be gently rounded, not rising to a high dome.*

Finishing touches

4 Tie the stems with twine, then cut the stem ends level. Place two sheets of tissue paper on your work surface and then place the bunch diagonally across the paper, with the stem ends toward the center. Draw up the corners and wrap the paper carefully around the bunch; then, in exactly the same way, overwrap the bunch with a sheet of cellophane.

Using cellophane over the paper not only creates a highly professional finish, but also adds sparkle.

In waiting

5 Shape the wide ribbon into a four-loop bow. Hold the bow at the center with your thumb and forefinger, and then tie around the center with the narrow ribbon. Tie this around the bunch and trim the ends into an attractive V-shape.

At this stage, you will not be able to put the flowers in water – nor even spray them – as the dye in the tissue paper would run. Instead, stand the bunch in a dry container such as a bucket, and keep it in a cool, dark place until needed.

Blackberry brambles bring a little of nature indoors in this unusual decoration. Arranged around a fluted ring mold, the brambles make a compact network that holds all the other plant stems very securely.

The wild look

What you need...

- Ring mold
- Florist's scissors
- Craft knife

Plant material
- Fruiting blackberry stems
- Purple sage
- Sweet marjoram flowers
- Mauve scabious
- Blue lisianthus
- Lime-green chrysanthemums
- Light and dark pink everlasting pea
- Lime-green miniature spray chrysanthemums

...and some tips!

- Container option
If you do not have a ring mold, use an ordinary round metal cake pan with a water-holding inner liner.

- Seasonal variation
You could combine yellow-berried holly stems with variegated sage and bay leaves, decorating them with sea holly (Eryngium maritimum) and yellow and mauve dahlias, for an attractive late-autumn decoration.

Forming a network

1 Arrange the blackberry stems around the ring mold so that the tips overlap the inner and outer rims at intervals, then cut off some of the leaves and rearrange these among the stems.

Make sure that the blackberry stems crisscross each other all the way around the ring to form a complex network, as this will make your task much easier as you add all the other plant material.

Complementary color

2 Tuck sprays of purple sage among the blackberries so that some also overlap the outer edge of the ring. Arrange the marjoram flowers, scabious and lisianthus flowers around the ring, distributing the textures, shapes and colors to best advantage.

Avoid putting many strong-colored flowers together: a concentration of the deep blue lisianthus, for example, might resemble a dark hole in the arrangement.

Cluster of interest

3 Use the craft knife to split the green chrysanthemum stems so that they can take up water, then arrange them in a cluster, where their sharp green color will become the focal point. Position short sprays of the miniature chrysanthemums opposite and around these chrysanthemums. *The miniature chrysanthemums will help to provide color balance and create a unified appearance.*

Finishing touches

4 Finally, use sprays of light and dark pink everlasting pea to fill in any gaps. *The untidy growth of this wild-looking flower is well suited to informal arrangements – in this case, to one that begins with brambles!*

Rich harvest

What you need...

- Wood basket
- 2 white candles of different heights
- Florist's clay
- 2 plastic florist's prongs
- Florist's scissors
- Water-holding vials (optional)

Plant material
- Selection of vegetables such as butternut squash, eggplant, pepper, zucchini, chili pepper, and pattypan squash
- Sunflowers
- Trails of hops
- Clematis stems with flowers and seed heads
- Passion flowers

...and some tips!

- In hot water *Sunflowers especially will benefit from proper conditioning before you start to arrange them (see pages 134–5).*

- Seasonal variation *Orchard fruits – rosy apples and pears – would make an attractive harvest-time group. Passion fruit and lychees would also look eye-catching if combined with roses and some trailing ivy.*

A wood basket loaded with richly colored and textured vegetables, bright sunflowers and trailing hops is transformed into an eye-catching harvest-time candleholder.

Candle power

1 Attach the candles securely to the
wood basket, with space between them:
press a strip of florist's clay on to the flat
side of each set of prongs and adhere to
the bottom of the basket. Then press
the candles into the prongs. Arrange the
vegetables all around the candles.
*Make sure that both the basket and
candles are completely dry before
using the clay, or it will not adhere.*

Water source

2 Condition the sunflowers if necessary (see opposite). Cut the stems to
varying lengths – some so short that
they will rest on top of the vegetables,
and at least one much longer so that it
will appear to grow out of them. Push
the stems into water-holding vials.
*For a short-term decoration you
can arrange the sunflowers just as
they are, but using the vials will prolong the life of the composition.*

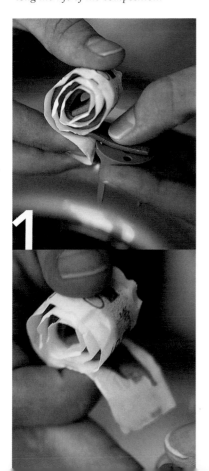

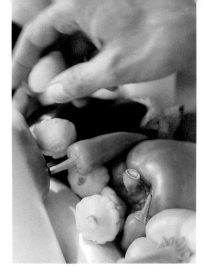

Concealment

3 Place the sunflower stems (in the water-holding vials) among the vegetables, and rearrange the squash, peppers and so on, as necessary, to conceal the water holders.

You can angle the vials in any direction – even horizontally – as the hole in the cap closes tightly around each stem and will prevent seepage.

Natural curves

4 Add trails of hops and clematis stems to ramble over the vegetables, around the base of the candles and across the rim of the wood basket. You can also fit these stems into water vials but, if you are not using these, the stems will simply dry out naturally and still look attractive.

As you add these elements to the decoration, you will see that gradually the vegetables play a less important part, and eventually just form a colorful background for the flowers, hops, foliage and seedheads.

Finishing touches

5 Lastly, add the passion flowers. These will benefit from a moisture source so, if you don't have vials, fill small plastic pillboxes or tiny bottles with water and pierce a hole in each lid to hold the stems.

Notice how the intricate coloring of the passion flowers links all the different hues of the vegetables, from the reddish-purple of the eggplant right through to the creamy yellow of the butternut squash.

Berry bright

What you need...

- Block of florist's foam (to fit inside the basket)
- Bowl
- Rectangular basket with moisture-proof inner container
- Florist's scissors
- Kitchen knife

Plant material
- Peony leaves (or similar large foliage)
- Sprays of rowan berries
- 1 globe artichoke
- Pink and orange Peruvian lilies
- Hypericum (St. John's-wort) berries
- Orange and bronze zinnias

...and some tips!

- Preparing stems
You will need to condition the woody rowan stems before you arrange them (see pages 134–5).

- Maintenance
Remember to keep the florist's foam permanently moist by filling it up with fresh water each day: there are a lot of thirsty stems in this arrangement!

In a porch, on the floor, in the corner of a room or in an alcove: wherever you decide to put this bright decoration, it will help to herald the arrival of winter.

1

Preparation

1 Soak the florist's foam in a bowl of water for about 20 minutes (or until it sinks), and then place it in the moisture-proof container in the basket. Begin the arrangement by positioning the peony leaves (or similar foliage) to make a fan shape across one end of the basket. *While the florist's foam is soaking, condition the woody rowan stems (see pages 132–3).*

Vegetable flower

2 Cut the stem of the globe artichoke at a very sharp angle, so that you can easily press it into the foam without breaking it up. *You are using the artichoke in place of a large, focal-point flower, so show it to advantage by gently opening it with your fingers to reveal its more colorful inner leaves.*

A straight diagonal

3 Position long sprays of rowan berries diagonally across the basket. *Adding the sprays of shiny berries in this way helps to create extra textural and directional interest.*

Working in clusters

4 Arrange clusters of Peruvian lilies within the outline created earlier with the peony leaves, and fill in any gaps with sprays of hypericum berries. *As you insert the lilies you will appreciate the contribution of the berries – their color picks up the dark flashes in the lily petals, while their texture contrasts well with the softness of the flowers.*

Closing the gaps

5 Finish off the arrangement by positioning the bright zinnias in a ring around the artichoke head. *Turn the basket around and check that the florist's foam is completely hidden from every angle. Although the foam does serve an invaluable purpose in an arrangement of this type, it is very ugly to look at!*

In 30 minutes

Gift posies

What you need...

- Shallow bowl
- Colorless cellophane, cut into 8-inch squares
- Transparent tape
- Scissors
- Glass vase
- Wine glasses (optional)

Plant material
- Selection of flowers and foliage such as delphiniums, Brompton stocks, roses, lisianthus, ice plant, green (unripe) poppy seed heads, variegated sage, carrot leaves or fern fronds and variegated ivy

...and some tips!

- Color change
Have fun with color: wrapping posies in colored cellophane (for instance, yellow flowers and foliage in red cellophane) will create an intriguing illusion of floral colors that do not exist in nature.

- Seasonal variation
This is an idea for all seasons, and you can use it with numerous combinations of flowers and foliage – the only restrictions being what you can find and what works well.

Tiny posies of romantic, pretty flowers and pale, pastel foliage are beautifully wrapped and would make charming gifts – perhaps as mementoes of a family celebration.

1

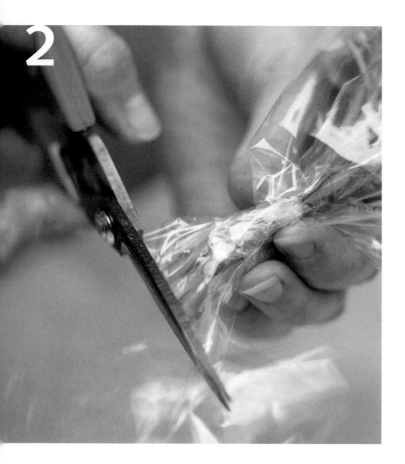

Color balance

1 Make your selection of flowers and foliage to compose the first posy, gathering the materials up in your hand so that you can assess the effect of the varying colors and textures. For a vibrant posy full of interest, you will want to contrast flowers borne on short spires with fully rounded ones, and solid colors with variegated ones. Place all the ingredients for the posy crosswise in the center of a cellophane square. Readjust the stems so that none of the flowers will be obscured, and then carefully wrap the cellophane to form a loose cone around them.

Secure the overlap of cellophane with a strip of transparent tape, keeping this as unobtrusive as possible.

Water course

2 Cut off the end of the cellophane cone and then place the posy in the bowl of water in a cool, dark place. *The posy will spend the rest of its life out of water, so it is important to keep it fresh for as long as you can.*

Looking cool

3 Make up as many more posies as required, each time putting them into water to keep fresh.

To compose an all-green posy that contrasts with the more colorful ones, select materials with striking texture and shape contrasts. For example, green poppy seed heads, lady's-mantle flowers and umbrella-shaped heads of ice plant can be blended with carrot leaves and variegated herbs, making a posy to prove that color does not always rule – although care in selecting the plant materials is essential.

Underwater

4 Press one of the posies below the water level in the display vase and see how it shimmers! Arrange more posies in the vase, facing this way and that, and check that all the flower and foliage stems reach into the water.

Another idea – in addition to the vase – is to flatter each guest around a party table by placing a single posy in a wineglass beside each setting. Choose a combination of plant materials to coordinate with the table setting or as a reflection of a larger centerpiece, or use flowers that are specially meaningful to you.

The full circle

What you need...

- 8 inches florist's foam ring
- Sharp knife
- Shallow bowl
- Florist's scissors
- Skewer
- Plate or dish (for display, optional)

Plant material
- Small-leaved ivy.
- Orange marigolds
- Orange, bright pink and yellow roses
- Variegated pineapple mint
- Green poppy seed heads
- Ice plant
- Delphinium buds
- Chives
- Lady's-mantle

...and some tips!

- Aftercare
On completion, mist the flowers with cool water. Remove the wreath to a water-resistant surface and spray it at least once a day, or twice in hot weather. Keeping the foam ring moist will also prolong the life of the arrangement.

- Seasonal variation
For a Christmas or Thanksgiving wreath, cover the foam ring with mixed ever-greens such as juniper, ivy and bay, and decorate it with small red and bronze spray chrysanthe-mums and rose hips.

A floral wreath – traditionally a symbol of hospitality and welcome, but often confined to Christmas – is used here to make a long-lasting table decoration; it could also be hung on a wall or a door.

Sizing down

1 Some preformed foam rings have unnecessarily thick bases. If you wish to cut down your ring to a more manageable size, use the sharp knife to slice through the base. There is also a practical reason for this, because it will take considerably less foliage and flowers to conceal the foam structure. Soak the ring in cold water for 20 minutes. Meanwhile, prepare all your flower materials by cutting the stems short – to approximately 2½ inches – and putting them in a shallow bowl of water.

At this stage you may find it helpful to arrange the flowers in color groups, as you will be using them.

Foliage first

2 Arrange curving trails of ivy over and around the sides of the foam ring until you have almost covered it. *The leaves not only provide a natural framework against which the flowers will be viewed, but also go a long way toward concealing the foam.*

Block of color

3 Use the skewer to make holes in the foam, then insert marigold stems so that the flowers create a patch of vibrant color on the ring.

Positioning some short marigold stems horizontally – with the flowers nestling closely against the inner and outer rims of the ring – will do a good cover-up job.

Rose bed

4 Create neighboring patches of roses in contrasting colors (you will not need a skewer to make way for these much tougher stems).

As you work around the ring, insert stems at varying angles so that the flowers face in different directions, just as they would grow naturally.

Cool interlude

5 Create a cool area of pineapple mint, poppy seed heads, ice plant and delphinium buds to contrast strikingly with the vivid fiesta colors of the flowers; clusters of chives tied in knots and inserted among the herbs and seed heads will add height and visual interest. Add short sprays of lady's-mantle to fill in any gaps through which the foam ring is visible, turning the arrangement around to check it from every viewpoint.

If you intend to use the wreath as a table decoration, place it on a plate or dish to prevent the moist foam from marking your furniture.

In the style of an Old Master painting, this composition brings together flowers in a wide range of tints and shades spanning more than a single season.

Dutch influence

What you need...

- Deep, round bowl
- Block of florist's foam
- Sharp knife
- Florist's scissors
- Craft knife

Plant material
- Sprays of foliage
- Blue delphiniums
- Apricot roses
- Magenta dahlias
- Pink and orange Peruvian lilies

...and some tips!

- Maintenance
Remember to keep the florist's foam moist by filling it up daily with water. With such a large number of stems drawing on the moisture, the foam would otherwise quickly dry out.

- Seasonal variation
In early spring, it would be lovely to combine evergreen foliage and the bright berries from the end of the winter with tulips, daffodils, hyacinth and year-round (greenhouse) carnations and spray chrysanthemums.

Preparation

1 Soak the florist's foam in a bowl of cold water for about 20 minutes (or until it sinks). Using the sharp knife, cut a slice from one end, then stand the main block on end in the bowl and wedge it in place. Arrange foliage stems all around the foam block, creating a narrow fan shape to define the eventual height and width. Cut some stems short and angle them forward and backward, at the front and back of the foam, to give depth to the arrangement. Arrange the delphinium stems among the foliage, keeping within the height and width boundaries already set.

The framework of pale green foliage and soft blue flowers makes a natural background, against which the rounded flower heads will be viewed.

Color distribution

2 Strip all the lower leaves from the roses and use the craft knife to remove any thorns, then position the stems within the arrangement.

In a massed display like this one, it is most effective to position some of the principal flowers facing out to the sides so that they are seen in profile.

Filling-in

3 Fill in the gaps with the dahlias and Peruvian lilies. Cut some lily flowers from the main stem and recess them in close against the foam, where they will help to cover it up. Turn the bowl around to check that the florist's foam is concealed from every viewpoint, and fill in any gaps if necessary.

Recessing the lily flowers in this way, so that they will be seen in shadow, gives perspective to the arrangement. The viewer is also aware of hidden depths, which provide greater interest.

A shallow bowl filled with a dome of golden-yellow dahlias and roses could be the center of attraction at any family gathering, from a golden-wedding celebration to a Thanksgiving party.

Golden bowl

What you need...

- Block of florist's foam
- Wide, shallow bowl
- Florist's clay
- Kitchen knife
- 2 plastic florist's prongs
- Florist's scissors
- Craft knife

Plant material
- Smokebush foliage (or greeny-yellow or lime-green foliage – not plain dark green leaves)
- Golden dahlias
- Rudbeckia seed heads (or teasels or yellow thistles)
- Yellow roses
- Orange Peruvian lilies

...and some tips!

- Waste not...
Do not be afraid to cut the smokebush stems short. You need not waste the lower leaves – put them at the back of the foam, angled backward. They will give depth here, and no one will see their lack of leafy tips.

- Seasonal variation
An all green-and-white arrangement would be dramatic in a green bowl: try combining sprays of rosemary and white-flowering jasmine with white camellias and green hellebores.

Preparation

1 Soak the florist's foam in cold water for about 20 minutes (or until it sinks). Cut strips of florist's clay and stick them to the flat side of the two prongs; make sure that the bowl is thoroughly dry, then press the clay-lined side of the prongs into the bottom of the bowl. Cut the foam to fit, then press it on to the prongs. Cut smokebush stems to varying lengths and arrange fanlike around the foam.

The tallest stem at the center will define the eventual height of the arrangement, and the shortest ones at the sides will determine the width.

Keeping within bounds

2 With the foliage in place, all that you have to do now is to follow the outline you have set. Position the tallest dahlia in the center, close to the tallest foliage stem, then continue arranging the golden flowers around the bowl.

Step away from the arrangement as it takes shape to make sure that you are keeping to the rounded dome form. This is not a decoration that will tolerate any wayward stems!

Light touch

3 Arrange groups of the spiky orange rudbeckia seed heads among the dahlias, with some stems angled forward to create width and perspective. *Notice how these beautiful orange flower centers (which remain on the stem once the petals have fallen) catch the light in myriad ways – they are a real bonus in this arrangement.*

Roses all the way

4 It is now time to arrange the roses. Strip off all the lower leaves and use the craft knife to remove any thorns, then position the roses between the dahlias, still working within the overall outline. Cut the Peruvian lily flowers from the main stems and position them among the principal flowers, close against the florist's foam, where they will conceal it very effectively.

Even the most beautiful blooms sometimes have discolored petals, but don't let any blemishes spoil your arrangement – gently pull off any damaged outer petals and the flowers will be perfect again.

Finishing touch

5 Turn the bowl around slowly so that you can assess it from every angle. *If you spot any unsightly gaps, fill them in with short sprays of smokebush leaves or any leftover lilies.*

Techniques

Flower holders

Try to think laterally as you choose the containers that will do most to flatter your choice of flowers and foliage. You are likely to find just the thing in the least expected places. Pitchers and baskets, baking pans and casseroles, glass tanks and drinking glasses, teapots and flowerpots, fruit and even vegetables – all can play a role in creating the perfect partnership between container and plant materials.

When choosing a suitable container for a flower display, you do not necessarily have to be restricted by practical considerations. A container need not even be moisture-proof to display fresh flowers efficiently – in that case, you will simply have to fit it with a water-holding liner.

Plastic margarine tubs and yogurt pots are ideal for this purpose, but they are unsightly. Whenever a liner of this kind would show through the container – in an open-weave basket, for example – you can fill the gap between the two with a natural material such as moss or ivy leaves, or with a color-coordinated material such as crumpled tissue paper or even a piece of silk.

Secret ingredient *(right)*
This closely woven wicker basket becomes a practical fresh-flower container, having been fitted with a water-retaining holder. Check that a liner like this one is not visible from any angle and, if necessary, tuck a few extra leaves or seed head stems around the rim of the outer container.

Practical consideration *(above)*

A ring mold has two practical advantages in flower-arranging terms: the hole limits the area to be filled with stems, and also makes it easier to place the first stems so that they form a supportive mesh. A short tumbler or beaker placed in the center of an ordinary dish would fulfil the same functions.

Prearranged *(below)*

You can arrange flowers in a wide-necked container such as this kitchen pitcher in two ways. Either position the stems around the outside of the container first, crossing them over to form a network to support the central stems; or, as here, arrange the flowers in your hand before lowering them into the container.

High profile

Any vase with a narrow neck – such as the classic urn shape – is a real time-saver in flower arranging. You will find it quick and easy to position a few stems with confidence in a container of this kind, knowing that they have no room to move!

Complementary containers
(opposite page, top left)

Always think about the suitability of a container for the flowers you plan to put in it. For instance, the depth of pattern on this Greek-style urn would be distracting in juxtaposition to small, delicate blooms. Big, bold sunflowers, whose centers are a match for any deeply etched and sand-brushed swirls, make a much better choice.

Dual purpose *(above)*

Aluminium flower buckets, which are sufficiently deep to give flowers and foliage the long, cool drink that they need initially, also make the grade as containers at the display stage. Their clean lines and grainy texture will complement mixed-flower groups or all-of-a-kind displays, from the palest peonies to the darkest dahlias.

One for the pot
(opposite page, top right)

New teapots in clear, bright colors, or patterned ones with the romance of age (often to be found as garage sale bargains), make interesting containers. Here, the bright yellow of the teapot is echoed in the color of the lily, then contrasted with the mauve shades of the verbena posy.

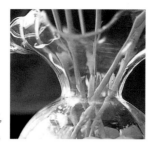

Below the waterline *(above)*

Add a handful of kumquats to a glass container before arranging your chosen flower stems, and you will create a new visual dimension as well as an element to steady the stems. You could make use of this idea but vary the effect by substituting summer-green peapods or small okra, autumn-brown walnuts or chestnuts for the kumquats.

Sharp choice *(below)*

Orange shells make delightful holders for small nosegays of flowers; you can change the color and aroma by using grapefruit, lime and lemon shells. Either scoop out a little of the flesh and press your chosen flower stems into what remains, or hollow out the shells completely; in the latter case, you could then fit small blocks of presoaked florist's foam into the larger fruit shells.

Clear option

The irregularly striped skin of a watermelon, in contrasting tones of green, is a perfect foil for both bright and pastel plant materials. At times and in places where watermelons are plentiful and inexpensive, you might like to press flower stems directly into this sunset-colored fruit; a more economical option is to scoop out the flesh and to fill the shell with an inner container or with a chunk

of presoaked florist's foam.

Salad days *(above)*

Chunks of fresh cucumber make surprisingly attractive and versatile flower holders: the two ends provide gradually tapered vases, while the sections cut from the center are straight and sturdy. Experiment with different ways of displaying these adaptable holders. One nice idea is to stand each one on a stout glass or china candlestick – or on a wooden candlestick, provided that you protect the surface beneath from moisture.

Stem treatments

Plant materials need care to accustom them to vase life. The way you harvest the materials – and even the temperature and time of day at which you do so – will affect their longevity.

If possible, gather flowers and foliage either early in the morning or in the evening – not in the middle of the day. Never snap off stems as this could damage the severed stem and the plant, but cut stems with a sharp blade or with florist's scissors. Cut at an angle to expose the largest area of plant tissue to the new moisture source (the water or soaked florist's foam in your arrangement). Make sure that all cutting, splitting and scraping tools are clean and sharp.

To condition most thin-stemmed flowers – such as snapdragons – strip off the lower leaves and place the stems in cool water. Thick stems – such as dahlias and sunflowers – need splitting at the ends so that they can absorb water; woody stems must be scraped at the ends to remove the outer tissue. Stems such as poppy and spurge, which bleed readily, need a further process: hold the ends over a flame until blackened, repeating this if you need to recut the stems.

Thirsty work *(right)*

As soon as possible after cutting the stems of flowers, foliage, bracts and berries, place them in a deep container of cool water (ideally, take a bucket with you as you gather plant materials in the garden). Then treat all the stems in the appropriate ways and put them in water again, in a cool place and away from strong light.

Stripping leaves

(opposite page, top left)

Strip all the lower leaves from flower stems before splitting the stem ends and standing them in water for several hours. Hold each stem – this one is a lily – firmly in one hand and run your other hand down the stem, stripping off all the leaves in a single movement.

One at a time

(opposite page, top right)

Removing large leaves from a stem such as hydrangea is quite simple. Hold the stem with the flower head facing you, and with your thumb against the stem, push each leaf sharply downward to snap it off.

Alternative choice *(above)*

Do not discard the hydrangea leaves that you have stripped away from the main stems – these can come in very useful for other purposes. To keep them fresh, cut off the nodules at the end of the stem and put the stems straight into cool water. These large, pointed oval leaves, with their prominent vein structure, are useful for providing visual weight when positioned close to the rim of a container or, alternatively, for adding extra depth and perspective at the back of an arrangement.

Tender care

Tender stems with supple leaves need handling with special care. Pick off leaves of this kind one by one, being extremely careful not to snap off the flowers as you do so, which can easily happen. For a small composition, separate the flowers from the main stem and arrange each individually.

Paring woody stems *(above)*

Scraping the woody tissue from stems cut from shrubs and other woody plants is vital to prolong vase life: hold a craft knife parallel to the stem, then scrape off the outer tissue all around the stem for about 2 inches.

Splitting thick stems *(above)*

After scraping the outer tissue from woody stems, and always before arranging thick-stemmed flowers such as dahlias, sunflowers and chrysanthemums, use a sharp craft knife to split the stem about 2 inches. This is an additional way of ensuring that the stems will be able to take up water readily and so will survive for as long as possible once in a vase.

Boiling-water treatment *(above)*

Immersing stem ends in boiling water prolongs life by removing air bubbles and killing bacteria; protect flower heads from the steam with a cloth.

A prickly operation *(below)*

Stripping thorns from rose stems is an optional extra to make them more comfortable to handle, but will be essential if you plan to compose a hand-tied bunch, posy or bouquet.

More to the point

You must condition woody stems just as carefully as other stems. Cutting the ends at a sharp angle is best when you are using florist's foam; the pointed stems will pierce the holding material more readily and so are less likely to break it up.

Winter berries

Bright clusters of berries – such as rowan and hawthorn – add an interesting textural contrast to flowers and foliage of all kinds. To prepare the berries, pare and split the stem ends, dip them in boiling water and then leave them in cool water; they should then stay fresh for several days.

On the slant *(below)*

To make sure that a free-standing bunch will be secure without support, you will need to cut the stems level but not straight across. Cut each one separately, at an angle, so that it will readily take up water when you eventually place the bunch in water.

Revival tactics

Foliage and flowers that have wilted in the sun, or have been out of water for a long time, can be revived by recutting the stem ends under water. Partly fill a bowl with water and, using florist's scissors, cut the stems just below the surface. As always, cut each at a sharp angle.

Total immersion *(above)*

Another revival technique, which you can use for robust and compact flowers such as roses, carnations and ice plant, is to plunge the flower heads upside-down in a container of cool water for a minute or so. Shake the flowers gently to dry them off, and then stand the stems in cool water before arranging them.

Stem supports

As many of the designs in the book show, you do not need to use any holding material to create a variety of natural-looking floral decorations. However, there are times when some kind of stem-holding device will give you even greater freedom to compose arrangements that are structured yet informal.

In some designs, it is possible to arrange the stems of the flowers and foliage that form part of the design crosswise, to act as a support system for other, perhaps heavier stems at the center. In other cases, trails of evergreen foliage such as ivy, or translucent leaves like hop or vine, are wound around the inside of a container to form a network to hold the arranged stems (this is very pretty in glass containers).

Other supports range from a simple framework of transparent tape or a tied triangle of cinnamon sticks to ready-made stem holders such as florist's foam; metal pin holders will also steady the heaviest stems.

Latticework *(right)*
You can fit any bowl or dish – however deep or shallow – with a crisscrossing mesh of transparent tape that will hold long stems upright or, if you cut the stems short, will support a patchwork of flower heads. Measure and cut the strips of tape to reach from side to side of the bowl or dish. Starting at one edge, pull each strip taut, take the ends over the rim and press them firmly in place. Continue placing parallel strips across the bowl from side to side, then complete the mesh by attaching parallel lines of tape at right angles to the first. The smaller the gap between the strips are, the longer the stems they will support.

Edge to edge

With the latticework of transparent tape in place (see page 134), you can create a variety of effects with short-stemmed flowers. Position them edge to edge to conceal the holding structure, in concentric rings or stripes of large or small flower heads, and in matching or contrasting colors. If you pour water carefully between the holes of the mesh and do not allow the tape to get wet, you will be able to reuse the structure again and again.

Heavy metal (above)

Pin holders are extremely useful devices: they are available from florists in a good range of shapes and sizes, and will take a firm grip on woody stems or on top-heavy plant materials. Made with thick, heavy metal bases and sharp, closely spaced pins, holders such as the one shown here should last a lifetime.

A firm grip

Unless a pin holder fits tightly into the base of the container that you intend to use for an arrangement, you will need to fix it in place with a strip of florist's clay pressed on to the underside (another option is to use modeling clay, although this is not waterproof and so will often be unsuitable). Secured in this way, a narrow pin holder such as the one shown above will provide very firm support.

A perfect triangle (page 135)

Three cinnamon sticks will contribute both stem guidance and aroma when you are arranging individual stems or flower clusters in containers such as drinking glasses or beakers. To make these unconventional holders, bind three equal lengths of cinnamon stick, bamboo or twig to make a triangle. Natural-colored raffia, coarse string or fine cord all make suitable ties.

Geometric pressure

You will be able to adjust the size of the aperture – and therefore the effectiveness of the triangular stem holder – by sliding the ties along the sticks to narrow or widen the gap as required. Flowers in strong, bright colors look especially good with these woody holders.

Using a foam wreath (above)

With a preformed foam wreath you can compose floral rings with all the charm of traditional welcome wreaths, and with the advantage of a built-in moisture source. In this way, fresh flowers arranged as table or wall wreaths will last as long as they would in any other floral design. Most rings are made of two types of synthetic foam bonded together: a top, absorbent layer that holds the stems and a bottom, nonabsorbent base. If you want to make the ring narrower and less clumsy, use a sharp knife to remove a slice from the base.

A good fit (above)

When using some containers – such as square or rectangular ones – it may be possible to wedge a block of florist's foam into them perfectly, with no need for anchoring. In a container such as this round bowl, however, the foam may need to be held steady with strips of florist's clay. The clay – which is extra tacky – can be pressed on to the base of a foam holder such as plastic florist's prongs.

Secure hold

With the florist's clay in place, the plastic prongs are pressed on to the base of the container, and then a cylinder or block of florist's foam can be pressed down on to it. When using florist's clay, you must ensure that both surfaces – the plastic prongs and the container – are thoroughly dry, or the clay will not stick (subsequent moisture will not dislodge it).

Effective cover-up

All types of florist's foam are practical but unsightly, and floral rings are no exception. Cutting a slice from the base of the ring (see above left) will help, by giving you a smaller area of foam to conceal. When you begin your arrangement, start by covering all surfaces of the ring with short sprays of foliage; these will not only act as a covering material, but will form a natural background for the flowers.

The right extension

Cutting the block of florist's foam so that it extends above the top of the container will allow you to angle some of the stems horizontally in line with the rim, and to slope others downward. Once the arrangement is finished, you will need to check it from every viewpoint to be sure that the foam is not visible.

Vertical precision (below)

Using florist's foam will give you the freedom to arrange a restricted number of stems even in a wide-necked container. With the sides of the foam block camouflaged by flowers and foliage, the design will also need some short-stemmed materials positioned so that they obscure its upper surface.

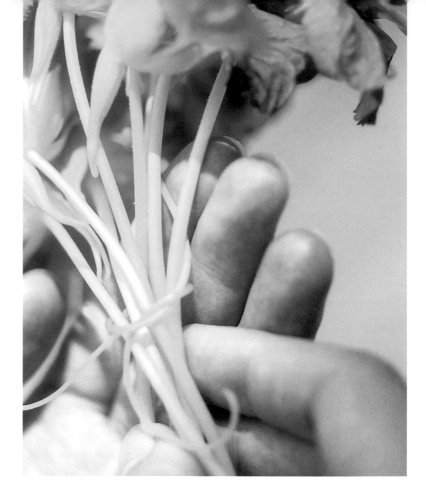

Shaping up

Hand-tied bunches, posies, nosegays – call them what you will, they have a charm that has been popular for many years. In Victorian times posies were exchanged as expressions of love, and today hand-tied bunches – with their crisscrossing stems – are favorites with amateur flower arrangers and florists alike.

Whatever style of posy you choose to make, it is important, more than ever, to give the flowers a good drink of water and to condition the stems (see pages 132–3), as they are likely to be out of water for some time.

Victorian posies were surrounded by a ring of leaves, to protect and frame the flowers. Ivy, lady's-mantle, scented geranium and violet are among the many leaves that will make a pretty final touch for a posy.

Most posies and hand-tied bunches are composed to form a gently rounded dome shape. To achieve this gentle slope from the center to the sides, each successive layer or ring of flower heads is placed just below the previous one, which avoids any risk of overcrowding or crushing the flowers.

Opening out *(right)*
The focal point of a flower arrangement, or the central flower around which you arrange a formal posy, should be perfect. If your chosen bloom – such as this lime-green chrysanthemum – is not yet fully developed, give nature a helping hand by gently easing out the petals all around the flower to create a more rounded shape.

Practical and pretty *(above)*
A tiny posy can be composed for display together with larger flowers in a teapot. This posy is tied with natural-colored raffia to hold the stems in position, before it is added to the arrangement. Raffia is a very useful material for flower arranging: it is pleasing to the eye, and so can be left visible if required. It is also practical, because it has a soft and pliable texture that will not easily cut through flower stems, even if it is tied fairly tightly.

Showing off
(opposite page, top left)
You can display this kind of posy, which has the charm and grace of a childhood composition, in many ways. For example, you could arrange several posies of similar or varying colors in a basket with a water-holding container fitted inside, or display them in a group, placing each posy in its own wine glass.

Natural ties
(opposite page, top right)
Nasturtium stems are among the most supple – and vulnerable – of all plant materials, and would almost certainly be cut through by a tie made of string or cord. Here the stems are bound with vine tendrils, which hold them gently and seem to be at one with the flowers.

Casting the dye
To some flower arrangers, the burnt-umber-colored stamens of the lily are a strikingly attractive feature; to others they are a nuisance factor. If you wish to avoid the chance of coloring the petals, your clothes or furnishings with their almost unremovable yellow dye, hold the flowers upside-down and snip off the stamens with scissors.

A flat-backed posy *(above)*
Before putting together a flat-backed posy that will be displayed without a moisture source – hanging on a wall or a bedpost, perhaps – you must take special care to condition the flowers properly. Having done this, arrange the flowers in your hand, using the longest stem in the center and making each successive layer slightly shorter.

At cross purposes *(above)*
A modern hand-tied bunch is composed of a multitude of stems arranged to cross about halfway along their length. Begin with two stems crossing over each other to make an X-shape. Give them a quarter-turn

in your hand, add two more crossing stems and continue in this manner until you have incorporated all the plant material.

Full circle *(below)*
When you wish to grace an arrangement with gently curving hop stems, or other stems with a similarly wayward habit, exaggerate the natural curves by twisting the stems into a wide circle. Leave them for a few seconds before unwinding them and they should spring into pleasing arcs.

Gentle curves *(below)*
The long, slender leaves of bear grass or pampas grass, both of which are long lasting in water, make an effective contrast of form and shape in arrangements of all kinds. To increase their natural curves, wind the leaves around your hand (or around a household item such as a jelly jar or tumbler), and wait for a few seconds before releasing them. Always handle these leaves carefully, or wear gloves – they have very sharp edges.

Modern interpretation *(below)*
A posy may consist of a single flower type, or of plant materials with widely differing forms, colors and characteristics. A wrapping of cellophane (with or without tissue paper beneath) will help to protect the flowers and to draw attention to their vibrant colors.

A clear message
You must keep the water that is needed to nourish cut stems clean, clear and cool. Murky water, which contains bacteria, will not only shorten the vase life of plant materials but, in a glass container, will detract from the appearance of the arrangement.

Nourishment

The vase life of cut stems will be determined by their conditioning and by their aftercare once arranged. Moisture is the principal requirement, and flower food – designed to replace the plants' own nutrients – is an optional extra.

Make sure that cut stems in any arrangement have an ongoing water supply. Fill up the water level, and make sure that it is always clean. If it looks cloudy or has an unpleasant smell, it needs changing completely.

Presoak florist's foam in water for about 20 minutes (or until it sinks); a brick-sized block will absorb about 3 pints of water in that time. Even this will not be enough to support a multitude of flower and foliage stems over several days, so you must keep the foam permanently moist.

Check that all containers and any other decorative elements that come into contact with cut stems are scrupulously clean and can-not contaminate the water.

Spray your arrangements with a fine mist of cool water from a plant sprayer once a day; you will need to do this twice or even more frequently in particularly hot and humid conditions.

The finishing touch (right)
Wrapping a posy or hand-tied bunch in cellophane not only protects the flowers and foliage, but also adds a glamorous sheen to the composition. If you intend to display the flowers in their wrapping, carefully cut away the cellophane at the base of the posy so that the stems will be able to readily take up water.

Stage management
(page 140, top left)
Keep your flowers in water at every stage: as soon as you have cut the stems, after you have conditioned them (see pages 132–3) and while you are creating the arrangement. Here, nasturtium flowers have been left in a container of cool water before being used to make posies.

Individual needs
(page 140, top right)
Use water-holding vials like this one when you wish to arrange individual flowers or small clusters of stems in containers that are not moisture-proof, or when you want to give the impression that flowers are simply tucked in among fruit or vegetables in a bowl. These plastic vials provide stems with an individual moisture source that you can easily conceal among the other decorative materials in a group; they are available from florists.

Store-cupboard option *(page 141)*
Using store-bought flower food is not the only way to prolong vase life: you can stir 1 teaspoon of granulated sugar into each pint of water to provide cut stems with nutrients. To prevent bacterial growth, you can also add 1 teaspoon of regular-strength household bleach to the water (do not use this solution in arrangements that could come within the reach of young children).

Cool, clear water *(above)*
Spraying cut flowers, foliage and other plant materials with a fine mist of cool water will help to keep them fresh. Use a spray mister, as shown (these are available from florists, garden centers, and other specialty stores), or try a laundry sprayer. To fill up the water level in a container – especially one that has a narrow aperture – you will need to use either a funnel or a watering can that has a long, thin spout.

Looking cool *(above)*
Drops of water lingering on petals and leaves after spraying have a refreshingly cool appearance, but make sure that they cannot drip on to furniture surfaces. Leave the arrangement on the kitchen counter until the water has evaporated, or stand it on a moisture-proof dish or tray.

Drying out *(below)*
You can use seed heads to dramatic effect in arrangements of fresh flowers and foliage, and poppy, love-in-a-mist and rudbeckia seed heads (shown here) will need no further nourishment. Leave the seed heads on the plants until they have almost dried out, then hang them in bunches in a cool, dry place. Brush the stem ends with clear, waterproof varnish so that they will not develop mold when you arrange them in water or presoaked florist's foam.

Flower food *(below)*
Adding a commercially prepared flower food – designed to provide the plants with nutrients – to the water before you soak a block of florist's foam or fill a container can help to prolong the life of cut stems. Follow the recommended proportions specified on the packet, and add more food to the water when you fill up the container or change the water completely.

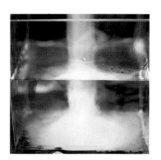

Index